written by Sierra Wilson & illustrated by Danika Runyan

REVELATION IS MY FLASHLIGHT

CFI • An imprint of Cedar Fort, Inc. • Springville, Utah

Sometimes life feels like the night.
I can’t see where to go.
But God gave me a special tool
To help me see and know.

The tool is revelation.
It's like a shining light.
The Holy Ghost points the way,
Showing me what's right.

Sometimes I can't see too far,
But I can see enough.
Revelation lights the way
Even when paths are rough.

Sometimes revelation comes,
Like a quick flash of light.
Sometimes it comes soft and slow,
Like dawn after the night.

Often, I see just enough
To take one step ahead.
As I ponder, pray, and trust in God,
It's by Him I'm led.

Revelation often comes
To both my mind and heart.
Thoughts and feelings guide me as
I strive to do my part.

Reading from the scriptures
Helps my flashlight glow.
The words of Christ teach me
The things I need to know.

Sacred music also helps,
And peaceful places too.
As I work to choose the right,
My light shines strong and true.

Church and the sacrament both
Keep my flashlight charged.
When I give my spirit fuel,
My light beams bright and large.

The light of revelation
Doesn't help only me.
God can show me how to serve
My friends and family.

Without revelation's light,
I'd stumble on my way.
I wouldn't see what's coming.
I'd struggle to obey.

But when I use my flashlight,
I'll see what is coming.
I'll see traps before I fall,
And walk past them humming.

Everyone needs a flashlight
To help them see their way.
The light of revelation
guides us home where we'll stay.

I'm so thankful for my flashlight,
A shining light of love.
Revelation is a flashlight
Sent from heaven above.

LEARNING RESOURCES FOR FAMILIES

WHAT IS REVELATION?

Revelation is the way Heavenly Father communicates directly with His children. He provides teaching, guidance, comfort, and knowledge through the power of the Holy Ghost.

HOW DOES REVELATION COME?

Personal revelation most often comes as warm, peaceful thoughts and feelings from the Holy Ghost. Personal revelation can also come as feelings of inspiration, clear ideas or words, feelings of comfort or strength, and even meaningful dreams.

SCRIPTURES ABOUT REVELATION:

"Ask, and it shall be given you; seek, and ye shall find; knock, and it shall be opened unto you: for every one that asketh receiveth; and he that seeketh findeth; and to him that knocketh it shall be opened" (Matthew 7:7–8)

"If any of you lack wisdom, let him ask of God, that giveth to all men liberally, and upbraideth not; and it shall be given him.

But let him ask in faith, nothing wavering. For he that wavereth is like a wave of the sea driven with the wind and tossed." (James 1:5-6)

"Yea, behold, I will tell you in your mind and in your heart, by the Holy Ghost, which shall come upon you and which shall dwell in your heart.

Now, behold, this is the spirit of revelation; behold, this is the spirit by which Moses brought the children of Israel through the Red Sea on dry ground." (D&C 8:2-3)

"Did I not speak peace to your mind concerning the matter? What greater witness can you have than from God?" (D&C 6:23)

"We believe all that God has revealed, all that He does now reveal, and we believe that He will yet reveal many great and important things pertaining to the Kingdom of God." (Article of Faith 9)

WHAT CAN WE DO TO PREPARE TO RECEIVE REVELATION?

- Faithfully pray and ask God
- Listen reverently
- Trust God and His timing
- Study the scriptures daily
- Seek to serve others
- Repent and keep the commandments
- Make peaceful time for gospel study and pondering
- Attend church meetings and partake of the sacrament
- Listen to peaceful music and visit holy places like the temple

GENERAL AUTHORITY QUOTES ON REVELATION:

"In coming days, it will not be possible to survive spiritually without the guiding, directing, comforting and constant influence of the Holy Ghost." (President Russell M. Nelson)

"Most frequently, revelation comes in small increments over time and is granted according to our desire, worthiness, and preparation." (Elder David A. Bednar)

"In the performance of our responsibilities, I have learned that when we heed a silent prompting and act upon it without delay, our Heavenly Father will guide our footsteps and bless our lives and the lives of others. I know of no experience more sweet or feelings more precious than to heed a prompting, only to discover that the Lord has answered another's prayer through you." (President Thomas S. Monson)

"The ability to qualify for, receive, and act on personal revelation is the single most important skill that can be acquired in this life." (President Julie B. Beck)

DISCUSSION QUESTIONS:

- How can revelation bless and help you in your daily life?
- How can revelation help you to bless and serve others?
- What can we do in our lives and homes to listen to the voice of the Holy Ghost and receive revelation?

ACTIVITY IDEA:

Practice walking through the house or completing an obstacle course when it is dark without a flashlight. Now try doing the same with a flashlight. Talk about how having a flashlight is like having personal revelation from God to guide our way.

For President Nelson, who inspired this story, and for every child who makes the world a bit brighter

—Sierra

ISBN 13: 978-1-4621-4574-4
ISBN 13: 978-1-4621-3135-8 (ebook)

Published by CFI, an imprint of Cedar Fort, Inc.
2373 W. 700 S., Suite 100, Springville, UT 84663
Distributed by Cedar Fort, Inc., www.cedarfort.com

Library of Congress Control Number: 2023938742

Cover design and interior layout and design by Shawnda T. Craig

Printed in China

10 9 8 7 6 5 4 3 2 1

Printed on acid-free paper